The Thrifty Kitchen

Wartime Lessons for the Modern Cook

1/23
2·50

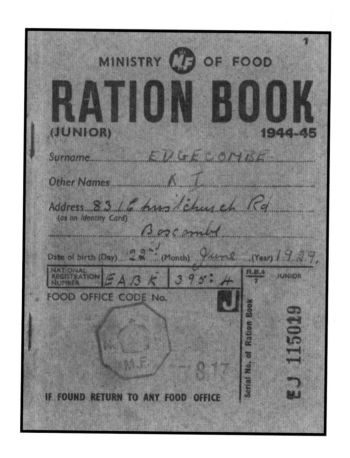

A cookery book in aid of Independent Age
With a foreword by Jane Fearnley-Whittingstall

The Royal United Kingdom
Beneficent Association

Supporting older people at home

Compiled and edited by Rebecca Law.

Design by Nikolai L'vov Basirov and Tim Rockel.

Food styling and photography (cover photographs and main intersection images) by Susie Mackie, www.susiemackie.com, susiemackie@btinternet.com.

Fork biscuits, lemon drizzle cake and scones by Sheina Donaldson, www.sheinadonaldson.co.uk, info@sheinadonaldson.co.uk.

Lemon curd by Dave Musson, www.davemussonphotography.com.

All other photographs by Paul Weekes or as indicated.

Printed by Butler, Tanner & Dennis.

Extract from *Fish, Meat, Eggs and Cheese Dishes* reproduced with the permission of *Good Housekeeping*.

Independent Age works to keep thousands of older people independent and out of poverty by providing them with practical support, financial help and lifelong friendship.

Independent Age, 6 Avonmore Road, London, W14 8RL
Tel: 020 7605 4200   Fax: 020 7605 4201
Visit our website: www.independentage.org.uk
Charity Registration Number 210729

ISBN 978-0-9562950-0-2

Mixed Sources
Product group from well-managed forests and other controlled sources
www.fsc.org Cert no. SGS-COC-005091
© 1996 Forest Stewardship Council
FSC

Contents

Foreword

By Jane Fearnley-Whittingstall

The time of this book going to print, September 2009, marks the 70th anniversary of the start of the Second World War. Shortly after the start of the war, rationing was introduced to ensure that everyone had their fair share of the limited resources available. Each person was issued with a ration book which allowed them just one fresh egg and three rashers of bacon a week. Anyone who was a child during and immediately after the war will remember sweet rationing as a deprivation. For our parents there was more at stake than chocolate, and the ration books were a prized possession. My mother kept hers in the drawer of the kitchen table, and out they came whenever she went to the shops.

For her and other cooks, culinary skills were tested to the limit, as they rose to the challenge of creating something interesting from whatever was at hand. In-season English vegetables and fruit, bread, flour, and oats were staple ingredients. Frozen pizzas, oven chips and the array of exotic imported food we take for granted today just didn't exist.

ousewives were proud to play their part in helping ith the war effort. Many, self-taught, embraced the rt of cooking enthusiastically. They used the limited sources ingeniously, respecting the available ngredients and avoiding waste. Above all, they were repared to put the time in to get a good meal out.

lowever, this was a matter of necessity rather than hoice, and it was with some glee that the members f the London Housewives' Association gathered in rafalgar Square on 4th July 1954 to burn a giant eplica of a ration book, in celebration of the end of ationing.

he Second World War certainly wasn't the first time n history that circumstances were hard and, of ourse, it was not to be the last. Seventy years later re find ourselves in the midst of an economic ownturn, bringing with it hardship for some families. he situation now can't be compared to that of rartime rationing, but many of us are having to ghten our belts. We are thinking more carefully bout what goes into our shopping baskets, and, hen it comes to planning budget-conscious and elicious meals, we could do a lot worse than seek aspiration from wartime cooks.

ince the war years our menus have been dramatically ransformed. Owing to the spread of global trade and he introduction of fridges and freezers we can cook ith virtually any ingredients at any time of year. But e have lost the pleasure of eating seasonal food.

on't be afraid this book will recommend stocking up n dried egg or Spam. You won't find a recipe for heep's head stew, where the teeth are left intact to smile up at you from your dinner. Nor will you find instructions for making such daunting fare as raw beef tea.

The book is, rather, about applying the principles of wartime cooking in a modern context, using modern ingredients. It's about the satisfaction of shopping sensibly and the enjoyment of observing the seasonal cycle of growth and harvest. If you buy fruit and vegetables when they are naturally in season they will be less expensive, not to mention tastier.

Some of the most delicious wartime dishes were created using leftovers, and the knowledge that not a scrap of food has been wasted will give you a warm glow of virtue rewarded. As well as being cost-effective, the wartime diet is considered one of the healthiest in history, owing to reduced consumption of meat, fats and sugar.

But the overriding reason for a return to cooking in this way is that fresh vegetables taste better than frozen ones, gently simmered stews made with cheaper cuts of meat are full of flavour, and seasonal dishes such as blackberry and apple crumble are treats to look forward to.

Introduction and Acknowledgements

The funds raised from the sale of this book will go to Independent Age, a charity committed to keeping older people independent and out of poverty by providing them with practical support, financial help and lifelong friendship. The charity focuses its support on those who are over 70.

This collection of recipes, some authentic from the war years, others entirely modern, has been sent to us by Independent Age beneficiaries, volunteers, supporters and friends. Plus you will find contributions from a number of celebrity chefs. We are extremely grateful to all of these individuals for their contributions to this book, which will help to raise funds so that Independent Age may continue its work, supporting current beneficiaries and spreading its reach to help more of the millions of older people who currently find themselves living in poverty.

Never a dull meal from now till the end of rationing – that should be the aim of every housewife who takes a proper, professional pride in her job. Supplies of body-building foods may be limited: foods may be available one day and vanished the next: time may be curtailed almost to the point of not existing at all and shopping difficulties multiplying every hour.

But difficulties are a challenge; and now, in wartime, the housewife has an opportunity she may never possess again to learn the real art of cooking. For the art of cooking consists not of putting together many sumptuous ingredients in the most expensive possible way. It consists of taking the ingredients at hand and using them with wit and imagination and skill. It consists of being alive to suggestions, ready to try out new dishes, eager to stock the larder shelves with every kind of seasoning and flavouring that present conditions have left in supply. It consists, above all, of being more ready to get up and try something new than to sit back and grumble about the lack of variety.

Taken from Fish, Meat, Eggs and Cheese Dishes, The Good Housekeeping Institute, 1944

Recipe Notes: Oven temperatures given are guidelines only as performance varies. Temperatures for fan-assisted ovens should be reduced by about 20°C from the one given in degrees centigrade.

Measurements are given in Metric and Imperial. Follow one set of measurements only, they are not interchangeable.

Seasonal Shopping

When it comes to food shopping, most of us have become used to being able to get hold of virtually anything we want at any time. That is really only due to the spread of global trade and intensive farming. Buying your raw ingredients when they are naturally in season is one way of saving on costs (because you are far less likely to be paying for them to be flown over from another country), and getting them when they are at their very best. Here is a basic guide to buying seasonally in the UK and Ireland:

January:
- Carrots, cauliflower, leeks, parsnips, squash, turnips, cabbage, celeriac
- Forced rhubarb, pears
- Goose, scallops, lobster

February:
- Leeks, parsnips, squash, turnips, swede, cabbage, cauliflower, celeriac, chicory
- Forced rhubarb
- Goose, guinea fowl, lobster, mussels, halibut

March:
- Carrots, leeks, purple sprouting broccoli, radishes
- Rhubarb, mint, parsley
- Lobster, sardines

April:
- Carrots, broccoli, cabbage, cauliflower, beetroot, radishes, kale, watercress, wild garlic, spinach
- Rhubarb, rosemary
- Lamb, cockles

May:
- Carrots, radishes, watercress, spinach, broccoli, cauliflower, asparagus, new potatoes, broad beans, spring onions
- Rhubarb, cherries, elderflowers, mint, parsley, rocket
- Lamb, duck, wood pigeon, sardines, sea bass, sea trout, lemon sole

June:
- Asparagus, broad beans, aubergines, peas, lettuce, courgettes, peppers, tomatoes
- Cherries, elderflowers, strawberries, gooseberries, redcurrants
- Welsh lamb, salmon, crab

July:
- Asparagus, broad beans, aubergines, peas, spinach, watercress, fennel, radishes, mangetout, French beans, new potatoes, cabbage, celery, tomatoes
- Strawberries, peaches, raspberries, gooseberries, loganberries
- Pigeon, clams, pilchards, trout

August:
- Aubergines, peas, lettuce, courgettes, peppers, sweetcorn, fennel, tomatoes
- Strawberries, greengages, raspberries, nectarines, peaches, loganberries, basil
- Hare, John Dory, crayfish, skate

September:
- Aubergines, sweetcorn, carrots, cabbage, cauliflower, parsnips, pumpkin, spinach, cucumber, onion
- Apples, blackberries, plums, damsons, elderberries, melons, pears, rhubarb
- Duck, venison, partridge, wood pigeon, grouse, sea bass, oysters, mussels, brown trout

October:
- Courgettes, marrow, pumpkin, mushrooms, beetroot, squash, watercress, kale, carrots, cabbage, lettuce, parsnips, potatoes
- Apples, figs, elderberries
- Partridge, grouse, guinea fowl, oysters, mussels

November:
- Pumpkin, beetroot, swede, parsnips, leeks, cabbage, potatoes, chestnuts
- Quinces, cranberries, pears
- Grouse, goose

December:
- Swede, parsnips, turnips, brussels sprouts, celery, celeriac, beetroot, red cabbage
- Pears, pomegranate
- Turkey, goose, sea bass

Soups
and
Starters

Cullen skink

Serves 4

Sarah Hartle

"I first tried Cullen skink when I was working in Aberdeen and it is a traditional favourite along that north east stretch of coastline. This traditional Scottish soup is essentially fish and potato. Made of 'finnan haddie' it's also the sort of simple, warming dish visitors might find at my (very independent) granny's croft on Orkney.

Cullen, named after the town in north east Scotland, and skink, meaning stew, is one of those sustaining soups best suited to windswept coastal locations.

The fish used should be the lightly salted, smoked, undyed variety – which is much more delicate than the orangey coloured variety we're used to encountering in English fishmongers, and definitely worth seeking out to get the full flavour of this dish."

450g/1lb undyed smoked haddock
Water
1 finely chopped onion
750ml/25 fl oz of milk
200g/7oz of buttery mashed potato
Salt and pepper
1 bay leaf
Small handful of chopped parsley to garnish

Skin the smoked haddock and cover with boiled water. Bring to the boil and then add the chopped onion and bay leaf.

Remove the haddock once it's cooked and remove the bones, but continue boiling the stock with the bones added for an hour. Then break up the fish into a dish.

Strain the stock and bring back to the boil. Boil the milk in a separate pot and then add to the stock along with the fish. Add the salt and boil for several minutes then add the mashed potato and stir to a smooth consistency. Add pepper and parsley to serve.

Sarah Hartley, online editor at the Guardian Media Group, has written the food blog *Life Through Food* since early 2006: http://sarahhartley.wordpress.com.

Pumpkin and lentil soup

Serves 4-6

Hugh Brown and Ros Jenkins

"If buying a whole pumpkin for this, then you may as well use the whole thing and store the leftover soup. It is very useful to get a strong person to deal with chopping the pumpkin. We normally make extra to give to Grandma for her lunches during the week. You can be approximate with measuring!"

1 tablespoon olive oil (for frying)
1 red chilli, seeded and chopped
1 onion
Coriander seeds, cumin (or whatever suitable spices are in the cupboard)
500g/1lb pumpkin, chopped (or butternut squash if pumpkin is out of season)
300g/10oz sweet potato, chopped
1½ litres/3 pints vegetable stock (or more if you'd prefer the soup thinner)
150g/5oz red lentils
1 tablespoon tahini (optional)
Coriander (if available)

Fry the chilli and onion until soft and fry the spices if you are adding any (don't let them burn). Add the pumpkin and potato and cook for about 8 minutes or so, until they soften. Add the stock and simmer for 5 minutes then add the lentils.

Simmer until everything is tender then blend (a hand blender is easiest, or transfer in batches to a food processor). Add tahini (optional) and heat before serving. Garnish with chopped coriander.

"Put the leftovers in a Tupperware pot and give to Grandma on the way home."

Darina Allen's Irish nettle soup

Serves 6

Darina Allen

"Stinging nettles grow in great profusion through the Irish countryside. Gather the nettles in the spring when they are young and tender and not too strongly flavoured. You'll need gloves to protect your hands. With their high iron content, nettles were prominent in Irish folk medicine and like many other wild foods they helped in some small measure to alleviate hunger during the famine among the older generation. The tradition of eating nettles four times during the month of May to clear the blood still persists. In fact herbalists confirm that nettles contain iron, formic acid, histamine, ammonia and siliac acid. These chemicals are known to alleviate rheumatism, sciatica and other pains. They lower blood pressure and blood sugar levels to increase the haemoglobin in the blood, improve circulation and purify the system so our ancestors weren't far wrong. In more recent times, nettles have become a much sought after ingredient for trendy chefs."

45g/1½ oz butter
285g/10oz potatoes
110g/4oz onions, chopped
110g/4oz leeks, chopped
Salt and freshly ground pepper
1 litre/1¾ pints chicken stock
140g/5oz young nettles
150ml/5 fl oz creamy milk

Melt the butter in a heavy saucepan, when it foams, add the potatoes, onions and leeks, toss them in the butter until well coated. Sprinkle with salt and freshly ground pepper. Cover with a paper lid (to keep in the steam) and the saucepan lid, and sweat on a gentle heat for 10 minutes, or until the vegetables are soft but not coloured. Discard the paper lid, add the stock, and boil until the vegetables are just cooked, add the washed and chopped nettle leaves. Simmer uncovered for just a few minutes. Do not overcook or the vegetables will lose their flavour. Add the creamy milk and liquidise. Taste and correct seasoning if necessary. Serve hot.

Darina Allen runs the Ballymaloe Cookery School in Ireland. She is a bestselling author, having written many books on Irish farmhouse cuisine and is a leader of the slow food movement in Ireland. She is the presenter of her cookery programme *Simply Delicious* on television in Ireland.

Curried parsnip soup

Serves 4

Pat Hammett, Independent Age beneficiary, Southampton

"Parsnips were a good wartime staple and were often used to fill out a family's sugar ration – they were sometimes used as a substitute for other ingredients, such as bananas, which were less readily available. Believe it or not, I cannot stand the taste of parsnips but, here in this soup, they are delicious. Do try it. It is fabulous."

60g/2oz low fat margarine
1 onion, chopped
1 large clove garlic, peeled and crushed
375g/12oz parsnips, peeled and diced
1 medium-sized potato
1 large dessert apple, peeled, cored and diced
1-1½ teaspoons mild curry powder
½ teaspoon turmeric
700ml/1½ pints of beef stock
Salt and pepper
1-2 tablespoons of low fat natural yoghurt
Toasted croutons to serve (optional)

Melt the margarine in a large saucepan, fry the onions, garlic, parsnips and potato for about 5 minutes, stirring frequently.

Add the apple and cook for a further 5 minutes, until the vegetables and apple are just tender. Stir in the curry powder and turmeric and fry for a further minute.

Make up beef stock with boiling water and add to the vegetables. Bring to the boil, turn down the heat and simmer for 15 minutes then leave to cool slightly. Purée the mixture in a food processor or liquidiser, or pass it through a sieve. Then pour the liquid back into the pan and reheat gently. Add seasoning to taste and stir in the yoghurt.

Serve immediately with croutons.

Pat Hammett

Pea soup

From Pat Hammett, Independent Age beneficiary, Southampton

15g/½oz butter
1 onion, finely chopped
1 potato, peeled and diced
340g/12oz frozen peas
1 litre/2 pints ham stock or water
Few sprigs of mint
Salt and freshly ground black pepper
85g/3oz cooked ham, chopped
4 tablespoons single cream

Put the butter into a large heavy saucepan, melt over a low heat and add the onion and potato. Leave to sweat for 10 minutes. Add the peas, stock (or water), sprigs of mint, salt and pepper. Bring to the boil then simmer slowly for 15 minutes.

Remove the soup from the heat and liquidise in a food processor or blender, then pass it through a sieve into a clean saucepan. Add the ham and reheat in the saucepan for 1-2 minutes. Add the cream and check the seasoning.

Serve immediately with white crusty bread.

Darina's wild garlic soup

Serves 6

Darina Alle

"In late April, the air in the top of Wilson's wood is heavy with the smell of wild garlic. Both the bulbs and the leaves of wild garlic are used in this soup and the pretty flowers are divine sprinkled over the top of each soup bowl."

45g/1½ oz butter
140g/5oz peeled and chopped potatoes
110g/4oz peeled and chopped onion
Salt and freshly ground pepper
900ml/1½ pints water or home-made chicken
    stock or vegetable stock
300ml/½ pint creamy milk
150g/5oz chopped wild garlic leaves

To garnish:
Wild garlic flowers

Melt the butter in a heavy-bottomed saucepan, when it foams, add the potatoes and onions and toss them until well coated. Sprinkle with salt and freshly ground pepper. Cover and sweat on a gentle heat for 10 minutes.

Meanwhile prepare the wild garlic leaves. When the vegetables are almost soft but not coloured add the stock and milk, bring to the boil and cook until the potatoes and onions are fully cooked. Add the wild garlic and boil with the lid off for approximately 4-5 minutes, until the wild garlic is cooked. Do not overcook or the soup will lose its fresh green colour. Purée the soup in a liquidiser or food processor. Taste and correct seasoning. Serve sprinkled with a few wild garlic flowers.

Friday night soup

Rebecca Law

"This recipe comes from a lady I stayed with when living in Holland. Kathy was a wonderful cook who had an amazing knack of making up something delicious from whatever she had in the cupboard. You can ake this soup so it's thick like a stew, or water it down for a more fluid consistency. Kathy called it Friday night oup but I make up a large batch and eat it right through the week."

1 slug of olive oil (for frying)
1 red onion, chopped
1 red chilli, seeded and chopped (optional)
2 x 400g (14oz) tins of good quality chopped
   tomatoes
1 x 400g (14oz) tin of kidney beans, drained
5 good handfuls of red lentils, washed
500ml-1 litre/1-2 pints water
1-2 tablespoons garam masala
1 tablespoon sweet Thai chilli sauce
Pepper to taste

To serve:
Coriander, ripped
Sour cream
Grated hard cheese
Jalapeño peppers
Tortilla chips

Fry the chilli and red onion in the olive oil until soft. Add the tomatoes and kidney beans and heat through for 2 or 3 minutes. Add 500ml/1 pint water and the lentils and bring to the boil. Add the garam masala and sweet Thai chilli sauce. Allow the soup to simmer for 15 minutes. You may need to add more water as the lentils soften and absorb the water. Cook until the lentils are soft.

Serve with your choice of sour cream, ripped coriander, grated cheese, jalapeño peppers and tortilla chips for dunking.

Leek and potato soup

Serves 4

From Pat Hammett, Independent Age beneficiary, Southampto

50g/2oz butter
1 tablespoon oil
6 leeks, cleaned and sliced
4 medium potatoes, peeled and sliced
1 litre/2 pints chicken stock
Salt and pepper
170ml/6 fl oz single cream
Chopped chives to garnish (optional)

Heat the butter and oil in a saucepan, add the leeks and fry for about 10 minutes or until softened.

Add the potatoes, stock, salt and pepper to taste. Cover and simmer for about 30 minutes or until the vegetables are tender. Cool slightly, then work in an electric blender until smooth, or rub through a sieve.

If the soup is to be served hot, return to the saucepan, add the cream and heat through gently; do not allow to boil. Adjust the seasoning if necessary.

Serve garnished with chopped chives.

Storecupboard fish pâté

Jacoba Oldham

"This pâté will keep for three days and can be frozen for up to one month."

1 tin sardines in oil (120g/4oz)
1 tin anchovies in oil (50g/2oz)
1 tin tuna in oil (185g/6½ oz)
Juice of 1 lemon
175g/6oz soft butter
1 small handful of fresh parsley
12 sprigs of dill
Ground pepper

Discard the oil from the tuna. Put the tuna into a food processor with the contents of the tins of sardines and anchovies (including the oil), butter, lemon juice, parsley and half of the dill. Process until smooth. Season with pepper and salt if you think it needs it. Garnish with the remaining dill. Cover and chill.

Salmon pâté

From Pat Hammett, Independent Age beneficiary, Southampton

1 large tin of salmon (use pink or red)
2 slices of white bread, crumbled
2 tablespoons mayonnaise
2-4 teaspoons white wine vinegar
Dash of pepper to taste

Drain all the liquid from the salmon. Scrape off the skin and remove the bones. Mash together with the breadcrumbs, using the mayonnaise and white wine vinegar to bind. Add pepper to flavour. Garnish with lettuce, cucumber, tomato and a lemon quarter.

You can use something like an ice cream scoop if you wish to make this into individual moulds.

Serve with brown bread, toast or melba toasts.

Richard Guest's simple pork pâté

Serves 10

Richard Gue

"Start the process for this two or three days in advance so it has time for the flavours to mature and the juices to settle."

500g/1lb pork neck or shoulder, diced
250g/9oz pork belly with no skin, diced
250g/9oz pure pork fat, diced
100g/3½ oz pig's liver, trimmed and diced
1 pig's kidney, trimmed and diced
½ nutmeg, grated
2 tablespoons garlic salt
2 tablespoons onion salt
3 tablespoons salt
5 tablespoons apple brandy
18 slices of dry cured, streaky bacon
150g/5oz pork fat diced into small cubes but not minced
3 bay leaves
12 twists of fresh ground black pepper

For the stock:
100g/3½ oz pork and bacon trimmings
1 small onion, peeled and chopped
2 bay leaves
Sprig of thyme
150ml/5 fl oz water

Plus: A 1 litre/2-pints capacity roasting tray

Day 1

Mix the pork neck, shoulder, belly, pure pork fat, liver and kidney with the nutmeg, garlic salt, onion salt, salt, apple brandy and black pepper. Mix well and chill overnight.

Lay a few strips of bacon on greaseproof paper and, with a rolling pin, roll out thinly. Line the mould so that the bacon ends meet in the middle of the bottom surface and there is enough overhang to pull over the pâté when the mould is filled. Chill until needed.

Make the stock by frying the trimmings and onion until brown, then add the herbs. Drain away excess fat and pour in the water. Simmer for 30-40 minutes. Allow to cook naturally, then strain and chill.

Day 2

Mince your marinated meats on a medium grind. Mix in the diced pork fat. Then mix in the stock thoroughly and adjust seasoning as required.

Richard Guest is currently the Head Chef at The Castle Hotel in Taunton, the Michelin Star restaurant which is regarded as one of the 20 top eating-houses in the country.

He is the author of *Jam with Lamb: Seasonal West Country Cooking* (published by Birlinn); a collection of recipes based on the very best of locally farmed and produced products.

Preheat the oven to 170°C/gas mark 3. Fill the mould, pressing the mixture down firmly making sure there are no air pockets. Fold over the bacon to anchor 3 bay leaves.

Half fill the roasting tray with boiling water that has an old tea towel in the bottom (to avoid the underside overcooking). Bake in the oven for 1 hour. Check with a skewer – if the tip is hot to your lip when inserted to the middle of the mould, remove to cool. If not, keep in the oven and check every 10 minutes until cooked. When cooked, remove pâté from mould.

Day 3+

Wrap the pâté in foil and keep in the fridge. To serve, cut into slices. Serve with Burcott Mill brown toast and Green Shed Apple and Date Chutney.

Tomato tart with basil and garlic

Serves 6-8 as a starter

Jacoba Oldham

500g/1lb puff pastry
450g/15oz (preferably large) tomatoes – taste
   is all important, so get the best you can
2 teaspoons of pesto
1 garlic clove, very finely chopped
2 tablespoons extra virgin olive oil
Fresh basil leaves
Salt and pepper

Roll out the pastry and cut out a single circle or individual smaller circles. Place on a greased baking sheet and prick the surface with a fork, leaving the edge free. Chill for 25 minutes. Bake in a preheated oven at 200°C/gas mark 6 for 20 minutes and then remove from the oven and allow the pastry to sink.

Dot the pastry with the pesto. Thinly slice the tomatoes and avoiding the top and bottom slices layer, slightly overlapping, on top of the pastry and pesto. Sprinkle with the garlic, salt and pepper and drizzle with olive oil. Bake for 5 minutes and then remove from the oven and sprinkle with torn basil leaves before returning to the oven for 5 minutes more until the tomatoes are cooked. Serve warm as a starter.

Green butter

Serves 4 *Jacoba Oldha*

"This recipe comes from my mother, 82-year-old Susan Graham, who lives near Ripon, North Yorkshire."

200g/7oz butter
2 anchovies
4 sardines
1 tablespoon chopped butter
Green colouring

Place all of the ingredients into a food processor until blended well. Spread the mixture into a toffee tray and cut into squares before refrigerating until firm. Remove squares from the tin and place on individual plates with a salad garnish. Serve with warm toast.

Cheese sables

Jacoba Oldha

"These delicious cheesy nibbles are another of my mother, Susan Graham's, recipes."

85g/3oz plain flour
85g/3oz butter
85g/3oz grated cheese preferably Cheddar
    (but a mixture will do)
Salt
Cayenne pepper
1 egg, beaten
Finely grated cheese to sprinkle on top

Put flour and seasoning into a food processor and gradually add the butter in small pieces. When well mixed, add the grated cheese. Chill for 30 minutes and then roll out thinly. Using a round pastry cutter stamp out biscuits and lay out on a baking tray. Paint the top of each biscuit with egg and then sprinkle on the grated cheese. Bake in a moderate oven for 10 minutes.

Meat, poultry and fish

Allegra McEvedy's gammon, leek and barley hotpot

Serves 4, handsomely

Allegra McEvedy

" Just to be sure, gammon is pork that has been cured, but not cooked yet - like bacon, but bigger. You don't need me to tell you you can do this with any veg you happen to have around, but it works best if you have representatives from each of the allium, brassica and root families. This is fine cold-weather eating: nutritious, warming and satisfying."

1½ litres/3 pints chicken stock, better fresh - tubs are fine, cubes less good
3 cloves garlic, peeled and chopped
2 heaped tablespoons chopped fresh thyme (or, failing that, 1 tablespoon dried)
2 bay leaves
1 large or 2 small leeks, sliced
3 carrots, sliced
A few leaves of cabbage - savoy works well
Half a small swede
4 x 200g/7oz slices gammon
170g/6oz pearl barley

Handful chopped parsley
Salt and pepper

In a saucepan heat the chicken stock with the garlic, bay, thyme and some seasoning.

Trim the fatty rind off the gammon slices and keep to one side. As the stock is warming, assemble your hotpot - I did mine in a round Le Creuset dish about 25cm across and 10cm deep, but anything deep enough that can sit on the hob is fine.

Allegra McEvedy, MBE has been a chef for 18 years, setting up a new concept in quality restaurants: that good food is something that should be available to all. In 2003, she co-founded Leon, the award-winning, healthy, fast-food restaurant group.

Allegra writes and broadcasts extensively, is the Resident Chef of *The Guardian's G2* magazine, and contributes a blog to the Observer Food Monthly. She is the author of three books, the most recent of which, *Leon: ingredients and recipes*, published by Conran Octopus, comprises recipes from the Leon restaurants.

Georgia Glynn-Smith

Put a scattering of leeks on the bottom, then about a third of the barley, then about a third of the gammon, some seasoning, a few round slices of swede, and so on and so forth until you have run out of space and/or ingredients: the most important thing is that you season well every couple of layers. Your ingredients pile can be a bit domed on top as it will collapse and compress as it cooks.

Pour on the warmed stock, scatter the gammon rinds and chopped parsley on top for added flavour, put a lid on and bring to a very slow simmer. Cook for about 45 minutes to 1 hour - it's done when all the veg and the pearl barley are soft.

Toss out the rinds and let it sit for a few minutes before serving with crusty bread and a good hit of mustard.

Gassie's "bittalion" stew

Serves 4

Jacoba Oldha

"Gassie (Great Aunt Sheila)'s Italian dish is known as 'bittalion stew' because it was cheap to prepare for feeding the Army officers' staff."

225g/8oz of macaroni
450g/1lb of sausage meat rolled into balls
225g/8oz tinned chopped tomatoes
1 x 400g (14oz) tin of tomato soup
2 onions

Cook the macaroni in boiling salted water until al dente. Slice the onions and fry in a little oil until golden brown. Place the macaroni, sausage-meat balls and fried onions in a casserole dish and add the tinned tomatoes. Season with salt and pepper and place in a medium oven for 45 minutes until the sausage-meat balls are cooked. Add the tin of soup and reheat before serving.

White stew

Caro Hart

"Here's a recipe from my Grandmother which I have always understood is from the wartime when they raised a piglet in the garden on kitchen scraps and then, when it was slaughtered, swapped half of it th another family for half of their sheep or lamb. Of course they grew their own vegetables. Even today, this very cheap to make.

is lovely on a cold winter's day and, in fact even better the following day (if refridgerated overnight) as the eat juices and starches from the root vegetables soak in even more and you get a lovely meaty 'stodge'!

easurements aren't given as they can be varied, depending on what you have available."

Potatoes, peeled and sliced
1½ kilos/3lb scrag end of lamb (you can use any
    cut but cheap cuts do very well)
Swede, cut into chunks
Carrot, cut into chunks
Optional root veg of your choice
Pearl barley
Lamb or beef stock

To serve:
Peas
Bread

Take a large casserole or slow cooker and layer with the potatoes, lamb and vegetables. Scatter pearl barley liberally across the top and then pour over the stock until it is just covered and the barley has washed into every corner.

Finish off with another layer of potatoes. Cook slowly on low (about 160°C/gas mark 3) for about 8 hours, uncovered for the last hour if the gravy needs reducing.

Serve with green peas and a hunk of bread for gravy and a handy bowl for the bones.

Bangers and roots

Serves 4

Jo Parfi

"My husband calls this 'root-te-toot stew'. My kids say this is the recipe they need to learn to take with them to university."

300g/10oz tasty sausages, Lincolnshire pork or Merguez are great (cut into chunks)

1 x 400g (14oz) tin of black or kidney beans (240g /8½ oz drained) or you can save more money by soaking 240g/8oz of dried beans overnight and then cooking until soft. (I love the taste of white soya beans in this dish)

400g (14oz) tin of lentils (or you can use 240g/8oz dried orange lentils straight from the packet)

1 red chilli (optional) finely chopped

1 large onion or 1 small leek, chopped

1 clove garlic, crushed and chopped

2 large carrots, peeled and diced

2 sticks celery, sliced

1 leftover stalk of brocolli if you have it, diced

300g/10oz of any root vegetables you like – sweet potato, swede, celeriac, parsnip, turnip or potato

2 tablespoons olive oil

400g (14oz) tin tomatoes, chopped

1 tablespoon cornflour

1 vegetable stock cube dissolved in 500ml/1 pint of boiling water

Take a heavy saucepan, casserole or frying pan. Fry the onion, chilli and leek in the oil on a fairly high heat for about 5 minutes until soft. Add the sausages and stir. Cook until coloured on the outside (about 5 minutes). Reduce the heat to medium and add the cornflour. Stir. Add the stock. Stir. Bring to a slow boil. Add the tomatoes and bring back to a slow boil.

Add the remaining root vegetables and bring back to a slow boil. Cover and simmer for 10 minutes or until the vegetables are al dente. Add the beans and garlic and return to the boil. Simmer, still covered, for 10 minutes.

Serve on its own or with chunks of bread, rice or couscous.

Jo Parfitt is the author of *French Tarts* (Octopus) and *Dates* (Zodiac Publishing). She lives in the Netherlands.

Scouse

erves 4 very comfortably

Barbara Park

" S couse is my regional dish; a meat-based stew, which was traditionally eaten by sailors throughout Northern Europe. It became popular in seaports such as Liverpool and remains a local staple there to his day.

's very cost-effective to make and was designed to use the cheap ends of meat."

225g/8oz stewing steak, cut into large cubes
225g/8oz lamb's breast, cut into large cubes
1 large onion, cut into large chunks
450g/1lb carrots, cut into medallions
2.3kg/5lb potatoes, peeled (450g/1lb finely diced, 1.8kg/4lb roughly chopped)
2 teaspoons of vegetable oil
1 litre/2 pints beef stock
Salt and pepper

To serve:
Crusty bread

Fry the meat in the vegetable oil until lightly browned. Transfer the meat to a large saucepan and add the onion, carrots and a fifth of the potatoes. Add the beef stock and season with salt and pepper. Let the pan simmer gently, stirring occasionally. The sauce will thicken as the potatoes cook.

Simmer for 2 hours before adding the rest of the potatoes, along with a few splashes of Worcester sauce. Then simmer for another 2 hours before serving.

Jane Fearnley-Whittingstall's risotto with chicken livers

Serves 3-4

Jane Fearnley-Whittingsta

"Whenever we had chicken, my mother made stock from the carcass. To intensify the flavour, she boiled the stock, reducing it until it was almost syrupy. With it she made soup or risotto. This was one of her best but had somehow been forgotten for several decades. I cooked it again recently. 'Very good. It's a cracker,' was the verdict."

225g/8oz chicken livers
Up to 600ml/1 pint good chicken stock
2 tablespoons olive oil, plus a little for the livers
1 onion, chopped
2 rashers of streaky bacon, diced
250g/9oz Arborio rice
½ glass of white wine
Salt and pepper
2 tablespoons chopped parsley and basil
115g/2oz Parmesan cheese

Cut the chicken livers into bite-sized pieces, removing any discoloured parts. Heat the stock in a saucepan.

In another large, heavy saucepan, cook the onion and bacon gently in the olive oil, until the onion is translucent. Add the rice and stir until it has absorbed the oil. Add the wine and let it bubble for a minute or two. (Don't leave out the wine, it really makes a difference.) Add enough hot stock to cover the rice and stir well. When the stock has been absorbed, add more, stirring from time to time to stop the rice sticking to the pan. After 20 minutes, taste the rice. If it is soft all through, it is cooked. If it is still a little gritty in the middle, continue adding stock and stirring.

In a small frying pan, fry the chicken livers gently in oil for just a couple of minutes. They should be pink in the middle. When the rice is ready, stir in the livers and chopped herbs. Add seasoning. Put the Parmesan on the table with a grater, for people to help themselves. Cheese bought in a piece has far more flavour than cheese sold ready-grated.

Variations: With a basis of good stock the risotto possibilities are almost infinite, including different combinations of meat, fish or shell-fish with various vegetables. Risotto can look rather grey and porridge-y, and a touch of green makes it more inviting. Try stirring in frozen peas near the end of cooking, or garnishing with chopped herbs, chives or finely sliced spring onion tops.

Tip: Some cooks put the risotto in the oven to cook after adding the stock, but if you want risotto with a really creamy texture, the stirring method on top of the cooker works best.

Jane Fearnley-Whittingstall is a grandmother of five and the mother of TV chef Hugh. She is the bestselling author of *The Good Granny Guide, The Good Granny Companion* and *The Good Granny Cookbook*. When not on duty as the Good Granny, Jane is also a successful garden designer, having secured two Chelsea Flower Show gold medals and penned a further seven books on plants and gardening.

This recipe is taken from *The Good Granny Cookbook*, her nostalgic exploration and rediscovery of the food our grandparents and great-grandparents used to make.

Jane Fearnley-Whittingstall's *Good Granny Cookbook* is published by Short Books.

Braised breast of lamb

Serves 6   *Kathleen Read*

A breast of lamb
2 onions, chopped
Your choice of vegetables such as 2 potatoes, a
  few French beans, carrots
Your choice of fresh herbs, such as mint, bay leaf,
  rosemary, parsley

To serve: 1 tomato, sliced

Cut the meat into chunks removing any surplus fat. Put it into a pan with the chopped onions and vegetables. Add the herbs. Fill the pan to cover the contents with cold water and add salt and pepper to taste. Simmer for 1 hour and then add a sliced tomato before serving.

Roast breast of lamb

Serves 3-4   *Kathleen Read*

A breast of lamb

For the stuffing:
170g/6oz white breadcrumbs
Grated rind of ½ a lemon
2 tablespoons chopped parsley
Chopped thyme
3 rashers of lean bacon, chopped
Salt and pepper
2 eggs, beaten

Plus: A little red wine for the gravy

Bone the meat and remove any surplus fat. Make a stuffing by combining the white breadcrumbs, lemon rind, chopped parsley, salt, pepper, chopped thyme and the bacon. Bind these ingredients together with the beaten eggs and mix well. Lay the stuffing on the laid-out breast of lamb and then roll up and skewer together. Roast for 45 minutes in the oven at 180°C/gas mark 4, basting from time to time with the red wine which will make good gravy.

Richard Guest's baker's potato with breast of salt marsh lamb

Serves 6

Richard Guest

"This is a hybrid between the French boulangière (translated into baker's) and Lancashire Hot Pot. As this dish uses salt marsh lamb and potatoes from Somerset, I call it Somerset Hot Pot."

2 salt marsh lamb breasts
2 onions, 1 halved and 1 thinly sliced
1 small sprig of rosemary
6 small or 4 large Maris Peer or Desiree potatoes, peeled
Salt and pepper

Preheat the oven to 175°C/gas mark 3. Cut the breasts in half and brown off each piece in hot fat. Make sure not to burn the bottom of the pan on too high a heat. When they are browned, mop away the fat from the pan with a paper towel and swill out the pan so as not to waste any flavour. Pour the liquid into an oven dish with the breasts, onion halves, rosemary and cover with water. Seal the pan with tin foil and a lid so no steam can escape and braise for 2 hours until the meat is falling apart.

Turn the oven up to 200°C/gas mark 6. In a dish big enough for six portions, slice some potatoes about 5mm thick and line the bottom of the dish with them. Season and sprinkle over some sliced onion and flaked lamb and repeat the process until the dish is filled. Pour over some of the cooking liquid, cover with foil and bake until the potato is soft.

Mark Hix's roast cauliflower with devilled lambs' kidneys

Serves 4

Mark H.

"Pan-roasting a thick slab of cauliflower is an ingenious way to serve it. Ray Driver, my old sous-chef at Le Caprice, came up with the idea some years ago and it went down a treat. You can use a piece of cauliflower like this as a base for all sorts of meaty dishes, but I reckon its caramelised sweetness is best suited to offal."

1 small cauliflower, trimmed
Salt and freshly ground black pepper
100g/4oz butter
Plain flour for dusting
14 lambs' kidneys, halved and trimmed

For the sauce:
4 shallots, peeled and finely chopped
6-10 black peppercorns, coarsely crushed
A good pinch of cayenne pepper
3 tablespoons cider vinegar
3 tablespoons water
40g/1oz butter
2 teaspoons plain flour
200ml/7 fl oz good beef stock
1 teaspoon English mustard
2 tablespoons double cream
8 small gherkins, finely chopped

Preheat the oven to 200°C/gas mark 6.
Cook the cauliflower whole in boiling salted water for about 8 minutes. Drain in a colander, then place under cold running water for a few minutes until cool; drain well. Trim the ends from the cauliflower and cut into four 1½ cm thick slices.

Melt half the butter in a frying pan until foaming. Meanwhile, dust the cauliflower with flour and season well. Pan-fry, in two batches if necessary, over a high heat for a couple of minutes on each side until nicely coloured. Then place in the oven to finish cooking for 10 minutes (if your pan isn't ovenproof or big enough, transfer the cauliflower to a roasting pan).

Meanwhile, make the sauce. Put the chopped shallots, peppercorns and cayenne pepper in a saucepan with the cider vinegar and water. Simmer gently until the liquid has almost totally evaporated, then add the butter and stir in the flour. Gradually

ark Hix has written a number of books on British
od. He has a passion for sourcing local food and
oking seasonally. He was the 2003 winner of
e Glenfiddich Newspaper Cookery Writer of the
ar award and was voted Best Cookery Writer by
e Guild of Food Writers in 2005.

e was Chef Director of Caprice Holdings Limited
r 17 years before opening Hix Oyster and Chop
ouse close to London's Smithfield Market and
ix Oyster and Fish House in Lyme Regis, Dorset.

is recipe is taken from his book, *British Seasonal
od*, published by Quadrille.

add the beef stock, stirring to avoid lumps
forming. Season lightly with salt and pepper,
and add the mustard. Simmer gently for 10-12
minutes. Add the cream and continue to
simmer until the sauce is of a thick, gravy-like
consistency. Add the gherkins and keep warm.

When ready to serve, season the kidneys. Melt
the rest of the butter in a heavy-based frying
pan. When hot, add the kidneys and cook over
a high heat for a couple of minutes on each
side, keeping them pink. Drain and add to the
sauce. Simmer for 20 seconds or so.

Pat the cauliflower dry with some kitchen
paper, then place a slab on each warm serving
plate. Spoon the kidneys and sauce on top and
serve straight away.

Jason Lowe

Egg and bacon pie

erves 3-4

Kathleen Read

For the shortcrust pastry:
170g/6oz self-raising flour
55g/2oz plain flour
70g /2½ oz margarine or butter
55g/2oz lard
Pinch of salt

Or 1 packet of readymade shortcrust pastry

For the Filling:
5-6 eggs
8-10 rashers of streaky bacon, cut into small dice
Black pepper

Plus: 1 egg, beaten

If you are making your own pastry: sieve the flour and salt together into a bowl. Add the fat, cut into small pieces, and rub into the flour with your fingertips until the mixture resembles breadcrumbs. Add just enough water to create a dough. Knead lightly until free from cracks and allow to chill for 20 minutes before rolling out.

Line a flan dish with half the pastry and place half the cut bacon on the pastry base. Break the eggs on top of the bacon singly and try to keep them whole. Gently spread the remaining bacon over the eggs and season with black pepper. Roll out the remaining pastry and make a lid for the pie, crimping the edges together well. Decorate with pastry leaves if desired. Make a small slit in the centre and brush with beaten egg before baking until nicely brown in a preheated oven at 190°C/gas mark 5 for about 40 minutes. Best served warm and great for a picnic type lunch.

Welsh faggots

Serves 4

Eve Saunde.

"This recipe is taken from Grandma Brown's scrapbook that I recently inherited."

560g /1 ¼ lb pig's liver
2 onions
100g/4oz fresh breadcrumbs
85g/3oz suet
3 level teaspoons of salt
2 level teaspoons of dried sage
540ml/1 pint boiling water

Mince the liver and onions and mix with the breadcrumbs, suet and sage. Use a tablespoon to create balls with the mixture and place them in a tin and cook at 180°C/gas mark 4 for 35 minutes. Pour the boiling water around the faggots and return to the oven for 5 minutes to allow a nice gravy to form.

Roman pie

Serves 4-6

Jacoba Oldha.

"This recipe makes a great cold lunch dish."

½ a cooked chicken, chopped into large pieces
A similar quantity of cooked macaroni
2 hard boiled eggs, chopped
2 slices of cooked tongue, chopped
1 shallot, chopped
Pepper and salt
500ml/1 pint boiled cream mixed with 3
    tablespoons reduced white sauce
115g/4oz grated Cheddar cheese

Layer all the ingredients together and bake for one hour in a bain-marie covered with tin foil.

When totally cold, cover with a layer of aspic.

Risi bisi

Serves 6

Lesley Browne, Independent Age beneficiary, Coventry

Our local supermarket sells cheaper own-brand bacon pieces. They also sell bacon pieces neatly cut into cubes but these are more expensive so we use the cheaper ones. I divide the packet into 100g portions and freeze them until I need to use them."

50g/2oz butter (or margarine)
1 onion
300g/11oz bacon pieces, chopped small
450g/1lb risotto rice
1litre/2 pints chicken stock
175g/6oz peas
225g/8oz Parmesan cheese

Melt the butter in a pan. Add the onion and bacon and fry for 5 minutes. Add the rice and stir to mix well. Pour in about a third of the stock and simmer until it has been absorbed. Add another third and continue the process until all of the stock has been used and the rice is cooked and tender. Stir in the cheese.

Lesley aged four

Peter Gordon's portabella mushrooms stuffed with goat's cheese and chorizo

Serves 4 as a starter or 2 as a main course   *Peter Gordon*

"This is a really simple lunch dish, or you could just serve one as a starter in the evening. They're also great served with a fried egg or two on top for brunch!"

8 portabella mushrooms
100g/4oz goat's cheese, crumbled or chopped
150g/5oz cooking chorizo, skin removed, roughly chopped
3 cloves peeled garlic, sliced
1 teaspoon fresh thyme leaves
2 tablespoons olive oil
1 cup fresh breadcrumbs (or use panko crumbs)
Salad leaves to garnish (I use pea shoots)

Oven at 180°C/gas mark 4. Sit the mushrooms on a board and carefully cut their stalk off at the base, then slice the stalks thinly and place in a bowl with the cheese, chorizo, garlic, thyme and half the olive oil. Mix it together until well incorporated, then rub the breadcrumbs in lightly to give you a crumble like consistency. Place the mushroom caps in a baking tin lined with baking parchment, gill side facing up. Divide the filling amongst the caps then drizzle the remaining oil over them and season generously with salt and pepper. Bake in the centre of the oven for 15-20 minutes, at which point the caps will have collapsed a little and stuffing will be sizzling away.

To serve: Place 2 or 4 caps on each plate, drizzling on any of the juices that have come off them and place some crisp, dressed salad leaves next to them.

Peter Gordon's hot-smoked salmon fish cakes with dill mustard dressing

Serves 4 as a main course

Peter Gordo

"Hot-smoked salmon has been cooked whilst it's been smoked – over a high to moderate heat. The flesh will look like poached salmon unlike the more familiar cold smoked salmon that is usually served sliced very thin and which looks raw or cured.

For 8 large fish cakes or 20 smaller ones – allow 2 large ones per main course, or serve the smaller ones as a starter or chunky canapé."

500g/1lb boiling potatoes, peeled and quartered
1 red onion, peeled and thinly sliced
3 tablespoons grain mustard
2 tablespoons sugar (brown or white)
1 tablespoon vinegar (any kind)
3 tablespoons coarsely chopped dill
4 tablespoons self-raising flour (plus extra for dusting the fish cakes)
250g/9oz hot-smoked salmon, skin and bones removed
A handful of roughly chopped parsley
Vegetable oil for cooking (or use butter and oil together)
Rocket or watercress for garnish

Put the potatoes and half the sliced onions in a pot and cover with cold water. Season with salt and pepper and gently boil until the potatoes are cooked. While they're cooking mix the mustard, sugar, vinegar and dill together and put to one side. Drain the cooked potatoes in a colander - making sure as much moisture as possible is drained off. Return to the pot and mash them then mix in the flour. Flake the salmon and add this along with the remaining sliced onion and the parsley and mix it all together. Taste for seasoning and adjust if necessary. Once it's cool enough to handle divide into either 8 or 20 fish cakes – then roll into balls. Flatten them into barrel shapes then dust generously in more flour. Heat up a pan and add 4mm oil (or a mixture of butter and oil) and when it's hot begin to cook the fish cakes. Gently flip them over when golden and cook on both sides. If you're making a lot of these it may be easier to colour them in the pan then cook on a tray lined with parchment in an oven set at 180°C/gas mark 4 until warmed through – around 5-8 minutes depending on their size.

To serve: place the fish cakes on warmed plates and garnish with the rocket, then dollop some of the dill mustard to the side.

Peter Gordon's smoked salmon and goat's cheese omelette

Serves 1

Peter Gordon

"This is a perfect supper dish when you have barely any time to make a full meal. You can use either hot smoked or cold smoked salmon, and the goat's cheese can be replaced with some feta and cottage cheese mixed together. A 20-24cm (8-9 inch) non-stick pan works best for this."

3 large eggs
A handful of flat parsley leaves
2 knobs of butter or 1 tablespoon of olive oil
50-80g/2-3oz smoked salmon, sliced or flaked
40g/1½ oz goat's cheese, crumbled

Crack the eggs into a bowl and add the parsley and 2 tablespoons of cold water. Season well with sea salt and freshly ground black pepper then using a fork beat the eggs for barely 3 seconds to break the yolks. Put the pan on to a medium high heat then add the butter or oil and when it's smoking pour the egg mixture in. Swirl it around a bit and use the fork to bring the set outer egg into the centre. After 10 seconds lay the salmon and cheese across the centre then leave for another 5 seconds. Carefully fold first one edge then the other over the filling then gently flip the omelette over so the seam is now on the bottom. Give it a few more seconds then slide onto a warmed plate. Serve immediately with hot buttered toast.

New-Zealand born Peter Gordon is co-owner and Executive chef of London's Providores and Tapa Room (www.theprovidores.co.uk). He is the author of several cookery books including *Cook at Home with Peter Gordon*; *World in my Kitchen*; *Salads - The New Main Course* and *Vegetables: The New Food Heroes*. He has appeared on various TV programmes on the BBC, Discovery, Channel 4 and the Carlton Food Network, as well as on networks in New Zealand and the US.

Chicken and chorizo paella

Serves 4

Caroline Moy

" I love Spain and food with a Spanish influence. This paella can be made up more economically than a seafood version."

2 large chicken breasts, cut into small bite-sized pieces
110g/4oz cured chorizo, sliced
1 large onion, chopped
1 tablespoon paprika
1 teaspoon cayenne pepper (optional)
300g/11oz paella or risotto rice
Knob of butter
1 litre/2 pints hot chicken stock
1 red pepper, sliced
10 cherry tomatoes, halved
1 handful green beans, halved
1 handful fresh flatleaf parsley, chopped

Dry fry the chorizo in a large pan or wok. The chorizo will start to release its own oil and turn red in colour. Remove the chorizo from the pan (place it in a large bowl) and use the oil to fry the onion until it softens, adding in the paprika and cayenne pepper. Add the chicken and fry for 3-4 minutes. Remove this mixture from the pan and add it to the bowl with the chorizo.

Heat a large knob of butter in the pan and add the rice, stirring it to give it a coating of the butter before adding the stock. Simmer for 10 minutes, stirring consistently. Put the chorizo, chicken and onion back in the pan and add the red pepper, tomatoes and green beans. Continue cooking until the rice has become tender (about 10 minutes) and season if necessary. Stir in the parsley just before serving.

Bell Inn smokies

Kathleen Read

Serves 6

"This dish comes from a restaurant called The Bell at Aston Clinton, in Buckinghamshire, which was renowned for its food in the 70s. The recipe was one of its signature dishes and was a closely guarded secret until one of my friends became a shareholder and insisted that if he was to invest he had to have the recipe!"

4 small Arbroath smokies or 1 smoked haddock (aprox 340g/8-12oz)
4 tomatoes skinned and de-seeded
280ml/9½ fl oz double cream
Parmesan or Gruyère cheese
Black pepper

Poach haddock or warm smokies and bone and flake. Pour half the cream into individual ramekin dishes, cover the flaked fish and roughly chopped tomatoes, season with pepper, pour over the rest of the cream and sprinkle with grated cheese. Bake at 180°C/gas mark 4 for 20 minutes. Brown under the grill.

Consommé mousse

Serves 6

Kathleen Rea

1 can condensed consommé
2 packets Philadelphia cheese
1 teaspoon curry powder
1 jar of lumpfish roe or pimento red peppers
Chopped chives

Reserve 4 tablespoons of the consommé and blend the remainder of the soup with the cheese and curry powder. Pour into individual ramekin dishes and set in the fridge. Pour the remaining soup on top and set again in the fridge. Garnish with lumpfish roe or chopped pimento and chopped chives.

Marinated kipper fillets

Serves 4-6

Kathleen Rea

1 packet of frozen kipper fillets or fresh kipper
   fillets
1 small onion
1 bay leaf
140ml/¼ pint French dressing
Parsley to decorate
Brown bread and butter

Thaw (if necessary) the fillets and place in a dish. Cut the onion into very thin rings and spread over the kipper fillets. Pour over the French dressing and marinate for several hours, turning occasionally.

Drain the fillets and serve with a few onion rings only on top of each fillet, decorated with parsley and a little of the marinade. Serve with brown bread and butter.

Delia Smith's tomato and anchovy quiche

Serves 4

Delia Smith

"This has a lovely Mediterranean flavour and tastes very good eaten out of doors on a hot summer's day."

shortcrust pastry (if using ready-made, 250g/9oz)
tablespoon olive oil
medium onions, peeled and finely chopped
clove garlic, crushed
700g/1½lb tomatoes, skinned, deseeded and
  chopped
teaspoon Herbes de Provence
x 50g (1½oz) tin anchovy fillets
tablespoons tomato purée
tablespoons chopped parsley
large eggs
25g/1oz black olives, pitted and halved
tablespoons grated Parmesan cheese
seasoning

Preheat the oven to 180°C/350°F/gas mark 4 with baking sheet in it.

Begin by lining a 25.5cm flan tin with the pastry, prick the base all over with a fork and bake it for 15 minutes. Then remove it from the oven and increase the heat to 190°C/375°F/gas mark 5. Meanwhile, heat the oil in a medium-sized saucepan and cook the finely chopped onions and crushed garlic over a gentle heat until softened but not coloured. Then stir in the chopped tomatoes and Herbes de Provence, and cook, uncovered, over a fairly high heat until the mixture is reduced to a thick consistency and most of the excess liquid has evaporated. Now drain the anchovies, retaining the oil from the tin. Chop up 6 anchovies, then cut the rest in half lengthways and keep them on one side. Remove the pan from the heat and stir in the 6 chopped fillets, tomato purée and parsley; then beat the eggs together in a basin before stirring them into the tomato mixture. Taste and season if necessary. Now spread the mixture evenly in the flan case and decorate the top with a lattice-work of the remaining halved anchovy fillets. Scatter over the olives, then sprinkle the surface with the oil retained from the anchovy tin and finally with the Parmesan cheese. Now bake for 40 minutes until the filling is puffed and light brown.

This recipe is taken from Delia's *Frugal Food*, published by Hodder and Stoughton. *Frugal Food* by Delia Smith, 1976 and 2008, reproduced by permission of Hodder and Stoughton Limited, an Hachette UK company. Author's royalties from the sale of *Frugal Food* will go to the Catholic Fund for Overseas Development (www.cafod.org.uk). For further Delia recipes and cookery information go to www.deliaonline.com.

Bachelor's pie

Madeleine Jon

"This dish is so simple it requires no educated measuring of quantities. When my husband and I first got together we had absolutely no money and it was a real struggle to get to pay day, so we came up with bachelor's pie."

Basically this is a dish of chopped potatoes layered with a purée of carrots and topped with either melted cheese or a cheese sauce depending whether there is milk in the fridge! It can be made more glamorous by the addition of crispy fried bacon bits and or Californian raisins to get a sweet and sour finish. Serve with baked beans or peas and you are soon up to three portions of veg!

Vegetables

Omelette ramekins

Serves 4

Ros Jenki

"These are one of the recipes we use when we have leftovers that need using up – we always seem to have eggs that need eating, plus a courgette and some carrots or sweet potato or similar. You can adapt this recipe to use whatever you've got!"

6 eggs
1 tablespoon milk
2 teaspoons plain flour
240g/8½ oz vegetables, cut into small cubes (1cm) (Whatever looks good, or is leftover in the fridge!)
¼ tsp nutmeg
250g/9oz frozen spinach, thawed
2 tablespoons grated vegetarian Parmesan (often labelled "Italian style hard cheese" in shops. If you can't find it, then leave it out – the recipe works just as well without)
Chunk of mozzarella, if required

You may also want to consider making a simple sauce to go with the ramekin – tomato and red wine, or mushroom and tarragon works well.

Whisk together the eggs, milk, flour, Parmesan and nutmeg. Squeeze excess liquid from the spinach and add to the mixture. You want the consistency to be fairly thick, well mixed and not watery.

Cook the vegetables to go in the middle – you could either steam it if you'd prefer it plain and are in a hurry, or roast them in a bit of olive oil with garlic and rosemary – you can really customise this as much as you like, depending on what you've got available.

Grease four ramekins. Pour the spinach mixture in until it is a couple of centimetres short of the rim. Spoon the vegetable mixture into the centre of each one (allowing it to sink). If you'd like mozzarella, then pop a small cube in the centre. Pour a little more spinach mixture over the top.

Cook in a moderate oven (170°C/gas mark 3) until set. Leave for a couple of minutes before turning out.

Lentil pie

Eleanor Carlisle

erves 4

" A s a vegetarian, I tried ways of coming up with simple and cheap recipes to get me through university. This is a recipe I remember my mum making when I was younger, It's a pastry-less pie that consists of st four ingredients."

450g /1lb red lentils
70g/2½ oz margarine
1 onion, finely chopped
85g/3oz Cheddar or other hard cheese, grated

Put the lentils on to cook in boiling water. Sauté the onion in a little margarine. When the lentils are soft, drain off any excess water and mix them with the cheese and margarine. Season to taste and turn the mixture into a greased, oven-proof dish and sprinkle with a little more cheese. Bake at 190°C/gas mark 5 for about 20 minutes or until brown and crispy.

Serve hot or cold.

Jane Fearnley-Whittingstall's gardener's pie

6 generous helpings

Jane Fearnley-Whittingsta

"This all-vegetable version of shepherd's or cottage pie is an improved version of an austere war-time dish, named "Woolton Pie" after the Minister for Food from 1940 to 1943. Lord Woolton's Pie attracted much mockery , but Alice Thomas Ellis's recipe, described in her book *Fish, Flesh and Good Red Herring* (Virago Press), is, in spite of its humble ingredients, not at all austere and makes a delicious lunch or supper dish, or as an accompaniment to roast lamb."

For the base:
1 kg/2.2lb of mixed winter vegetables, whatever is available, for example an onion, a celery stick, a large carrot, 2 Jerusalem artichokes, ½ a cauliflower, some swede
2 tablespoons olive oil
Stock or water
Salt and pepper

For the topping:
900g/2lb floury potatoes, peeled
50g/2oz butter
About 400ml/14 fl oz milk
115g/4oz grated Cheddar cheese

Set the oven at 220°C/gas mark 7.

Chop the onion and dice all the other vegetables into equal-sized pieces. Heat the olive oil in a wide, shallow saucepan and add the vegetables. Over the heat, turn them in the oil until they start to colour. Add enough stock or water to stop them sticking to the pan, and stir occasionally, until the liquid has evaporated. At this stage, the vegetables should still be crunchy. Season them to taste and put them in a pie dish. Don't worry if the mixture seems rather dry; the vegetables will release their juices during cooking.

Meanwhile, boil the potatoes and mash them with the butter, milk, cheese and plenty of freshly ground black pepper. Cover the pie with the mash and cook in the oven until the top is brown.

This recipe is taken from Jane Fearnley-Whittingstall's *Good Granny Cookbook*, published by Short Books.

Indian salad

erves 2   *Ros Jenkins*

"The recipe below is one of our summer staples for midweek evenings. It relies on things we're likely to have in the fridge/cupboard already, it's quick and also very moreish."

6 tablespoons olive oil
3 garlic cloves, sliced
2 red chillies, seeded, sliced very small
4 teaspoons cumin seeds, crushed
2 x 400g (14oz) tins of chick peas
3 tomatoes, seeded and diced
Zest and juice of 1 lemon
Naan bread (or you can use other types of bread if
    you don't have any naan)
25g/1oz coriander, shredded
½ cucumber, chopped into batons
1 red onion, finely sliced
100g/4oz spinach

Heat the garlic, chillies and cumin in some of the olive oil over a moderate heat for about ten minutes (don't burn). Add the chickpeas and heat for another five minutes (or until warm) and take off the heat.

Add the tomatoes and lemon to the chickpeas. Turn the grill to high, brush the naan with oil and grill until crispy on the outside. Tear into bite-sized pieces and toss together with the spinach, cucumber, coriander and red onion. Serve. Pour the chickpea mixture over the top of each serving.

The "A Matter of Life and Death" spicy sweet potato and black bean stew

Serves 3 to 4

Travis Elboroug

"Inspired by a dish that my American wife Emily's aunt kindly provided for such Turkey-avoiding vegetarians as ourselves during a Thanksgiving trip to Indiana, I felt compelled to fiddle around with some sweet potatoes and black beans when we got back to London. This is the make-and-mend result. And, fittingly enoug given the dish's origins and the film's transatlantic romance, we just happened to watch *A Matter of Life and Death* on the night that I first cooked it."

2 sweet potatoes, peeled and cut into chunks
A good dollop of extra virgin olive oil
1 large onion, chopped
1 large red, yellow, or even green pepper, sliced and deseeded
1 fresh chilli, chopped and deseeded, or 2 dried chillies, broken up, or a small teaspoonful of chilli powder
1 clove of garlic, finely chopped
2 x 400g (14oz) tins of tomatoes
1 x 400g (14oz) tin of black beans, drained - you can substitute pinto or even kidney, if you can't find black beans
The juice of 1 lime or a small lemon
500ml/1 pint of vegetable stock
1 heaped teaspoon of ground cumin
½ a teaspoon of paprika
A small teaspoon of honey or ½ a teaspoon of brown or granulated sugar
Generous shakes of salt and grinds of black pepper

First, fry the onion until softened in the olive oil in a large pan. Add the sweet potatoes and after 3 minutes or so, bung in the peppers and chilies, stirring the whole lot as you go and adding a dash more oil if it needs it, until they too have gone soft. Then bung the garlic into the pan and after about a minute or so, the tins of tomatoes, the cumin and the paprika. Stir in about half of the stock and keep it simmering for five minutes before tipping in the lime juice and then the honey. Season with salt and pepper and add the can of black beans and most of the remaining stock. Turn the heat down quite low now and leave it to bubble away uncovered for about 10 to 15 minutes, stirring occasionally. Ideally you want it to reduce so that it is fairly chunky, like a normal veggie chilli, say. Serve with rice and/or flat bread.

Travis Elborough is the author of *The Bus We Loved: London's Affair With the Routemaster* (Granta Books, 2005) and *The Long-Player Goodbye: The Album From Vinyl To iPod And Back Again* (Sceptre 2008).

Butternut squash and goat's cheese parcel

erves 3 to 4   *Rebecca Law*

M y boyfriend, Paul, stumbled across a recipe similar to this when flicking through a women's weekly magazine while waiting in the doctor's surgery. He's a keen cook but not a follower of recipes, so when rrived home from work the same day, found his own version baking in the oven."

tasty tomatoes (vine or organic), cut into chunks
00g/1 lb of butternut squash, cut into cubes
 large red onion, cut into large chunks
50g/5oz of goat's cheese
 egg
0g/2½ oz spinach
 packet of puff pastry sheets
aprika
live oil
alt and pepper

ut the squash, tomatoes and red onion in a oasting tray. Drizzle with a little olive oil and season ith paprika, salt and pepper. Roast at 160°C/gas nark 3 for about 20 minutes, until all the vegetables ave softened.

Meanwhile, cut up the spinach and goat's cheese. When the vegetables have cooked, put them into a mixing bowl, gradually adding the spinach and mixing in with a wooden spoon. Then crumble in the goat's cheese, again mixing all together.

Lay out a sheet of filo pastry and spoon the mixture into the middle, taking care not to overfill. Place another slice of pastry over the vegetable mixture and seal the two sheets together, crimping with your thumb and forefinger. Place the parcel on a lightly-oiled tray. Cut several lines into the pastry across the top. Brush the pastry with a beaten egg.

Bake for 30 minutes at 200°C/gas mark 6. Leave to stand for 5 to 10 minutes after cooking, before serving.

Enjoy with a crisp salad.

Puddings and desserts

Great Aunt Sheila's chocolate pudding

Jacoba Oldham

This recipe comes from my great aunt Sheila (Mrs Allen Hill from Beaminster, Dorset). It's a great children's favourite."

¼ loaf of white bread
55g/2oz butter
55g/2oz caster sugar
1 heaped teaspoon of cocoa
2 eggs, separated
280ml/9½ fl oz of water

Remove the crusts from the bread and discard (or make into breadcrumbs for another dish). Cut the bread into cubes and put into a saucepan with the butter, sugar, cocoa, water and egg yolks. Heat slowly until the butter is melted and then add the egg yolks. Pour the mixture into a buttered oven-proof dish. Whip the egg whites until stiff with half the sugar and then fold in the second half. Spread this meringue on top of the chocolate mixture and cook in a slow oven (150°C/gas mark 2) for 1½ hours.

Ming's chocolate mousse

Serves 4

Paolo Bra

"This is traditional fare from my step-gran, sadly no longer with us. This recipe dates back from the mists time and was most certainly served to my stepmother by her mum when she was growing up in a family of eight in early 1960s Salisbury."

4 eggs
225g/8oz bitter chocolate

Separate the egg yolks and the egg whites. Melt the chocolate in a bowl over hot water. Whisk the egg whites until they become stiff. Beat the egg yolks into the chocolate. Carefully fold the chocolate mix into the egg whites.

Tip the mixture into individual ramekins, chill lightly and serve.

Grandma's chocolate cake

Sara Campb

100g/4oz self-raising flour
100g/4oz caster sugar
25g/1oz cocoa powder
1 egg
100g/4oz margarine

Mix all the dry ingredients in a bowl, add the egg, then beat in the margarine until it reaches the consistency of soft, thick, cream. (If it stays too dry and won't cream up, add a little milk.)

Grease a cake tin (or line with greaseproof paper) and add the mixture. Cook in a preheated oven at 180°C/gas mark 4 for 20 minutes.

Canary pudding

Serves 4

Paul Weekes

This recipe comes from my mother, Christine. She made lots of different cakes when I was younger, but this was always my favourite. Most often, it's served hot with jam or golden syrup and custard, but I like it best served cold from the fridge when it has become harder in texture and I can eat a hearty slice with my fingers, with a glass of cold milk."

170g/6oz butter or margarine
170g/6oz caster sugar
170g/6oz plain flour
1 level teaspoon of baking powder
3 eggs
Rind of one lemon

Plus: 1½ pint pudding basin

Beat together the butter and sugar until creamy. Beat in the eggs gradually, add the lemon rind and stir in the flour and baking powder. Pour the mixture into the pudding basin and cover with a layer of greaseproof paper, tied with string. Place the bowl in a pan of boiling water and steam for 1½ hours. Top up the water throughout if needed. Serve with jam or golden syrup and custard.

Baked rice pudding

Serves 4

Rebecca La

" A friend of mine made this up for me one night when I was living in Hamburg. Needless to say, she was English and had brought this recipe with her. On a night that was -16°C and snowy outside, this pudding came as a welcome and very warming reminder of home."

1 tablespoon melted butter
115g/4oz pudding rice
55g/2oz caster sugar
850ml/1½ pints full-fat milk
½ teaspoon vanilla extract
40g/1½ oz unsalted butter
nutmeg

Preheat the oven to 150°C/gas mark 2. Grease a 1.2 litre/2-pint baking dish with the melted butter, place the rice in the dish and sprinkle with the sugar. Heat the milk in a saucepan until almost boiling – don't allow the milk to burn – and then pour it over the rice. Add the vanilla extract and mix everything together well.

Cut the butter into small chunks and scatter over the top together with some freshly grated nutmeg – enough to give it a good dusting.

Place the dish in the oven and bake for 1½-2 hours until the pudding has gone golden on top.

Marmalade pudding

erves 4

Susie Mackie

"My grandmother, Nanna, used to make this, and I loved it so much that when I left home I copied it from her handwritten recipe book into mine. I wish I knew more of its origins, other than that Nanna had ritten, in brackets 'from 1912'.

y to use homemade marmalade if possible, otherwise use a brand with a bit of 'oomph'! (I always use orange armalade, but I expect you could experiment with one of the many other flavours now available.) It is an timate comfort food pudding, especially with lashings of double cream!"

3 eggs
85g/3oz butter, softened
3 tablespoons orange marmalade
1½ tablespoons caster sugar
140ml/¼ pint milk
70g/2½ oz fresh white breadcrumbs

Separate eggs; beat the yolks, butter and sugar together until light. Beat in the marmalade. Taste and add more sugar if necessary.

Add the milk and breadcrumbs. Whisk egg whites until stiff. Fold the marmalade mixture into the beaten egg whites.

Pour into a buttered pudding dish. Bake at 190°C/ gas mark 5 for 40-45 minutes, or until well risen and golden on top.

Serve hot, with cream or ice cream.

Blackberry and apple crumble

Serves 4

Rebecca La

" As a child, my mother and I would quite often take a summer ramble on a Saturday or Sunday afternoon. Whenever we saw a blackberry bush bearing ripe fruit, it was just too much for my mother to pass it by. We'd collect the fruit in plastic bags, eating the plumpest, juiciest berries on the spot and returning home with give-away pink marks around our lips and on our fingers."

250g/9oz blackberries, washed
500g/1lb cooking apples, cored and cut into
   chunks
25g/1oz soft brown sugar
1 tablespoon water
1 pinch of cinnamon

For the topping:
75g/2½oz porridge oats
50g/2oz plain or wholemeal flour
40g/1½oz brown sugar
40g/1½ unsalted butter, cubed

Preheat the oven to 180°C/gas mark 4.

Put the apples, water and sugar into a saucepan and heat over a low heat, stirring frequently, until the apples become soft. Remove from the heat, allow to cool and gently stir in the blackberries and cinnamon and place the mixture into a pie dish.

To make the crumble, rub the oats, flour, sugar and butter together in a bowl until well mixed. Sprinkle this mixture over the fruit and bake for 30-45 minutes, until golden brown. Serve warm with custard or vanilla ice cream.

Tipsy roll

Serves 6-8

Kathleen Read

1 packet of Maryland cookies (or ginger snaps)
Sherry or brandy
280ml/9½ fl oz of double cream
Grated chocolate

Whip the cream until relatively stiff – but do not allow it to get too thick.

Dip the biscuits in the sherry or brandy and sandwich together with the whipped cream into a long roll. Cover the "log" with the remaining whipped cream and grate chocolate on top to decorate.

Grandma Weekes' sponge cake

Hugh Brown

"Going round to Grandma and Granddad's always meant one thing – making cakes! Grandma Weekes would write a shopping list and send Granddad and me round to the shops to get all the ingredients. Arriving back with the shopping, I was chomping at the bit to start making cakes, but Grandma and Granddad would always need their cup of tea first. With tea out of the way, I would set up the food mixer in anticipation, and hope that Grandma Weekes wouldn't scrape the mixing bowl out too thoroughly – leaving plenty for me to lick out afterwards!"

2 eggs
70g/2½ oz flour
70g/2½ oz sugar

Cream and beat the eggs and sugar well, then gradually add the flour, beating well. Put the mixture in a greased baking tray and bake at 180°C/gas mark 4 for about 20 minutes.

Mark Hix's Gooseberry and elderflower meringue pie

Serves 4

Mark H

" Some people find the sourness of gooseberries a bit off-putting, but they make really great desserts. Wit the exception of the red dessert variety, these berries need to be cooked with sugar. The elderflower gives them a complementary summery fragrance."

For the pastry:
2 medium egg yolks
225g/8oz unsalted butter, softened
1 tablespoon caster sugar
275g/10oz plain flour, plus extra for dusting
Melted butter for brushing

For the filling:
200g/7oz gooseberries
60ml/2 fl oz elderflower syrup (see over)
60g/2oz caster sugar

For the meringue:
2 egg whites
40g/1½ oz caster sugar

To make the pastry, beat the egg yolks and butter together in a bowl until evenly blended, then beat in the sugar. Stir in the flour and knead together until well mixed. Wrap the pastry in cling film, flatten and leave to rest in the fridge for an hour before use. Meanwhile, put the gooseberries, elderflower syrup and sugar in a pan over a medium heat. Cook, stirring every so often, for 5-6 minutes until the gooseberries have softened and the liquid has evaporated. Remove from the heat, cover with a lid or cling film and set aside.

Preheat the oven to 190°C/gas mark 5. Lightly brush 4 individual flat tins, 8-10cm in diameter and 3cm deep, with melted butter (or one large 20-23cm flat tin, about 4cm deep). Roll out the pastry on a lightly floured surface to a 3mm thickness. Cut out four discs (or one big one), large enough to line the flat tin(s).

This recipe is taken from Mark Hix's *British Seasonal Food*, published by Quadrille.

Line the tin(s) with the pastry, trimming away the excess just above the rims. The pastry is quite delicate but forgiving, so if it starts to break, just patch it up, moulding the pastry back together with your fingers. Crimp the edge for a neat finish, by pinching it between your thumb and forefinger all the way round. Leave to rest in the fridge for one hour.

Line the pastry case(s) with greaseproof paper discs, fill with baking beans and bake blind for 10-15 minutes until the pastry is lightly golden. Rest for 5 minutes, then remove the beans and paper. Turn the oven setting up to 200°C/gas mark 6.

Place the egg whites in a clean, dry bowl, making sure it is free from any trace of grease. Whisk, using an electric whisk, until stiff. Add half of the sugar and whisk for 2-3 minutes until the mixture is really stiff, then add the rest of the sugar and continue whisking until the meringue is very stiff and shiny. To assemble, spoon the gooseberries into the tart case(s), then either pipe or spoon the meringue on top to cover completely. Place on a baking tray and bake in the oven for 3-5 minutes until the meringue just starts to colour. Serve hot or warm.

Jason Lowe

Mark Hix's Elderflower syrup

Makes about 4 litres/7 pints

"This is a great standby for many desserts, ice creams and drinks. You can make it as strong as you like – just add more elderflowers to the infusion for a more intense flavour. If you want to make a syrup that's going to keep (like this one), then you will need to put in a fair amount of sugar to preserve it. Once made, simply dilute with fizzy or still water for a refreshing cordial, or try a splash in a glass of Champagne or sparkling wine for an aperitif."

1 carrier bag of elderflowers - about 800g-1kg
    (1.7-2.2lb), or 20 or so heads
1kg/2.2lb unrefined or granulated sugar
2 lemons, halved
4 litres/7 pints water

Remove any leaves and stems from the elderflowers and shake out any insects.

Place the elderflowers in a non-reactive pan with the sugar, squeeze in the lemon juice and add the spent lemon halves to the pan. Pour in the water, bring to the boil, then lower the heat and simmer for just one minute. Remove from the heat, cover and leave to infuse for 24 hours, stirring every so often.

The following day, strain the syrup through a muslin-lined sieve and stir into sterilised bottles. If you wish to keep it longer than a few days, then immerse the filled bottles in a pan of water, bring to the boil and simmer gently for 15 minutes then leave to cool in the water. Seal the bottles and store in a cool, dark cupboard.

This recipe is taken from Mark Hix's *British Seasonal Food*, published by Quadrille.

rene Betts' Christmas pud

ch pudding serves 8-10 people   *Jacoba Oldham*

I rene Betts is our old family cook. This was the recipe she used to make all the Christmas puddings for the family – now my job. But I add some gravy browning to the mixture before putting it into the bowls irred in well), to give it a good rich colour. I always make them in September so they can mature well – and it es me an opportunity to give them several top-ups of brandy, having skewered them all over so the brandy n sink in. They are very rich but quite well received on Christmas Day!"

15g/4oz self-raising flour
 teaspoon mixed spices and cinnamon
 teaspoon cloves
280g/10oz Demerara sugar
225g/8oz cooking apples
225g/8oz currants
15g/4oz peel
 glass of brandy
inch of salt
 teaspoon nutmeg
225g/8oz suet
The grated rind and juice of 1 lemon and 1 orange
225g/8oz grated carrots
340g/12oz raisins
225g/8oz sultanas
 tablespoons black treacle
 eggs, lightly whisked

Sieve the flour, salt and spices into a large bowl, add all dry ingredients and mix together. Melt the treacle in a pan, stir into it the lemon and orange juice, brandy and finally eggs. Pour the liquid into the pudding mixture, stir, cover and leave overnight. Put into 2x2 pint basins, cover and steam for 5-6 hours.

Jams, juices
and teatime treats

Grandma Brown's marmalade

Jenny Brown

G randma Brown was an avid writer, especially to the Bath Evening Chronicle, and loved nothing more than being interviewed, especially about her memories from when she was in service and wartime experiences. She was always delighted to have anything published and so would have been overjoyed to have her recipes in this cookbook."

4 Seville oranges 1 sweet orange 1 lemon 2.8–3.5litres/5-6 pints of water 2.2kg/5lb sugar ½ teaspoon cinnamon	Cut up the oranges and lemon and soak in the water for 48 hours. Also soak the pips, contained in a muslin bag. Boil the mixture (including the pips) for about 1½ hours until the orange and lemon rind is tender. Add the sugar and boil rapidly until the marmalade sets when tested on a cold saucer.

Josephine Henderson's lemon curd

Ian Gilbe

"My maternal grandmother raised a family through wartime rationing and post-war austerity, and the thought of buying preserves would have been anathema – on grounds of taste and cost.

As I became more adventurous in the kitchen, cooking became a shared interest for us. She passed on this recipe after marveling at photos of the lemon tree in our back garden when I lived in Australia. Make this once and you'll never again look at shop-bought lemon curd. It's dead easy – just remember to stir regularly or you'll get lemon scrambled eggs. Spread on your weekday toast or weekend croissants."

6 medium eggs
300g/10oz sugar
150g/5oz butter
Juice and grated rind of 3 large, juicy lemons
    (unwaxed if you can get them)

Lightly beat the eggs and place in an earthenware jug. Add the sugar, butter, lemon juice and rind and stand the jug in a saucepan of simmering water over a low heat. Cook, stirring regularly, until the curd thickens to about the consistency of custard (it will thicken as it cools). Pour into jars and allow to cool thoroughly before adding lids. Keep refrigerated and use within two weeks.

Manchester-based journalist Ian Gilbert turned his passion for cooking into a calling while working in Australia, where he was a contributor to Melbourne's *Age Good Food Guide* and compiled a weekly newspaper recipe aimed at the home cook.

Granny's apple chutney

Claire Nurd•

"This recipe belonged to my great-granny, Sue Tandy, who always had a glut of apples from her orchard."

1.8kg/4lbs apples
900g/2lbs dark brown sugar
225g/8oz sultanas
1 tsp ground ginger
55g/2oz mustard seed
1½ litres /3 pints vinegar (malt)
28g/1oz salt
28g/1oz onion

Cook all together for 2 hours stirring occasionally.

Old-fashioned lemonade

Kathleen Rec•

3 lemons
3 tablespoons sugar
940ml/33 fl oz of boiling water
Optional fresh mint to serve

Wipe lemons and cut into dice. Put into a jug with the sugar and pour on the boiling water. Leave for 15-30 minutes. Strain and cool. Add mint and ice before serving.

Lemon squash

Kathleen Read

5g/2oz citric acid (obtained from home brew shops)
00g/2lbs granulated sugar
ind of 3 lemons
litre/2 pints of boiling water

Put the citric acid in a bowl with the lemon peel and sugar. Pour over the boiling water. Cover and cool. Squeeze the lemons and add the juice to the bowl. Strain and keep in the fridge.

Elderflower cordial

Jacoba Oldham

This recipe comes from my mother, Susan Graham, and is perfect for the summer months."

5 Elderflower heads
5g/2oz citric acid (obtainable from home brew shops)
½kg/3½ lb caster sugar
.4 litres/2½ pints of boiled water
lemons – thinly sliced

In a pan make a syrup with the sugar and water and cool before adding the elderflowers, citric acid and lemons. Leave for two days stirring regularly and then strain and bottle. If strained into plastic bottles this can be frozen for longer-term storage.

Fork biscuits

Makes about 10-12 biscuits

Christine Mad

" I got this recipe from a friend of mine. Once we had both had children, we gradually lost touch but I alway thought of her whenever I ate these biscuits. Sending in this recipe spurred me onto finding her, which I did via the internet. I guess it must be ten years since we have spoken or seen each other but the fork biscuits being Debbie's recipe, have brought us back together again."

140g/5oz self-raising flour
115g/4oz margarine (not butter)
55g/2oz caster sugar
Vanilla extract (optional)

Preheat the oven to 175°C/ gas mark 3.

Soften the margarine and add in the caster sugar. Beat together until smooth and add the vanilla extract if desired. Add in flour and gradually work together.

Form into balls about the size of a walnut and press down on a baking tray with the back of a fork. Bake for 15-20mins until golden brown. When ready, the biscuits can also be dusted with icing sugar for better presentation.

These biscuits always fly off the plate, so you may want to double the quantities.

Scones

Rebecca L

" Scones are one of the first recipes I learned to make with my mother when I was a child. One of the overriding memories I have is of playing with the jam and cream combinations with my brother; whether it's best to lay a firm foundation with the jam first or go for the jam second to prevent ending up with cream o your nose!"

225g/8oz self-raising flour
Pinch of salt
55g/2oz butter
25g/1oz caster sugar
150ml/5fl oz milk
1 egg, beaten
50g/2oz raisins (optional)

To serve:
Butter
Good jam
Cream

Heat the oven to 220°C/gas mark 7.

Sift the flour into a bowl with the salt. Stir in the sugar and rub in the butter until you have a crumbly consistency. Stir in the raisins if you are using them. Add the milk, a bit at a time, and work the mixture into a soft dough.

Leave the mixture to rest for about 15 minutes before turning onto a floured work surface and rolling out to about 2cm/¾ inch thick. Using a round pastry cutter, cut the dough into individual scones. You should get 8-10 scones from this mixture. Brush the tops of the scones with the beaten egg, this will give them a shiny finish (or you can just sprinkle them with flour for a matt finish, if you prefer). Place the scones in the oven on a greased baking sheet and bake for about 12 minutes, or until they have risen and are golden.

Transfer to a wire rack and allow to cool before serving with butter, jam and cream.

Jane Plunkett's heart-shaped biscuits

Claire Nurden

"When my mother, Jane, got married, these biscuits were cut into heart shapes and served with strawberries and cream on her wedding day at Gretna Green. They were also in a jar in the newlyweds' room and served with every cup of tea. She loved the recipe so much that she asked the Sharrow Bay Country House Hotel, where they were staying, for the recipe before leaving."

450g/1lb butter
225g/8oz caster sugar
450g/1lb plain flour
225g/8oz brown rice flour

Cream the butter and sugar for five minutes. Mix in all the flour until bound together. Roll out and cut into shape. Bake in the oven at 150°C/gas mark 2 for 20-30 mins.

Easter biscuits

Hugh Brown

isits to Grandma and Grampy in Bath always included Sunday lunch. Their big dining table would be set up, filling the room as we all squeezed round. Being the youngest I would sit on my Grampy's organ stool I could reach the table! Still being in my pre-vegetable-eating stage, Grandma would cook spaghetti for me to with my roast dinner. At the end of the roast there was always great anticipation to see what Grandma Brown made for pudding... Would it be apple pie, would it be trifle? Of course at Easter it was even better as we w we'd also be getting Easter biscuits as well later in the afternoon – plus a big tub of them to take home!"

25g/8oz self-raising flour
15g/4oz sugar
15g/4oz margarine
5g/2oz currants
egg
teaspoon cinnamon

Rub the margarine into the flour, add the sugar, currants and cinnamon. Add the egg to make a stiff dough. Roll it out to ¼ inch thick and cut into round flutes. Place the biscuits on a baking tray and cook at 180°C/gas mark 4 for 20 minutes.

Great Grandma Caterina's fritelle

Enrico Spine

"Frittelle are carnival cakes that are prepared at home or found in patisseries in Italy. Common variations include 'semolina frittelle' or 'rice frittelle'. It is normal to bring frittelle or galani if you visit any home during carnival. This particular recipe was passed from my great grandmother, Caterina, to my granny, to my mum and now to me on a small, old, browning piece of paper. I was very proud to translate the recipe into English for this cookbook. I hope you will enjoy fritelle as much as I do."

100g/3½ oz potato starch (or corn flour)
500g/1lb plain flour
8 eggs
100g/3½ oz butter
Rind of 1 lemon, grated
200g/7oz sugar
½ teaspoon baking powder
1 pinch of salt
1 litre/2 pints of milk
250g/9oz sultanas
Cooking oil for frying
A double shot of grappa, rum or brandy

Put the flour and salt in a bowl and add the milk slowly, stirring continuously to avoid lumps forming. Put the mixture in a pan and heat slowly, bringing to the boil. Continue to heat for 10 minutes. When it thickens to the point that you can no longer stir it, place it in a bowl and allow to cool.

Add the grated lemon rind and the eggs, one at a time, kneading them into the mixture. Add the sultanas, liqueur, sugar and baking powder. This should create a sticky dough. Add more flour if the mixture is too wet.

Leave the mixture to rest for 8-10 hours.

To fry: fill a frying pan to three-quarters full with cooking oil and heat. Take a teaspoon of the dough and drop it slowly into the pan. Fry until the fritelle look golden (about 30-60 seconds), turning the fritelle in the oil. Remove the fritelle using a mesh basket and place them on a few sheets of kitchen towel. Keep adding and removing more fritelle, continuously, so the oil doesn't change temperature. To check if the fritelle are cooked, open one up to check it has cooked through.

After getting rid of the excess oil, place the fritelle in a bowl or on plates and sprinkle with icing sugar.

Galani

Makes about 90 galani

Enrico Spinello

"This recipe comes from my mother. We eat galani during carnival time, together with the 'frittelle'. They have many different names throughout Italy. They are called Galani in Venice (and in Padova, my home-town), bugie (lies) in Liguria and chiacchere (chats, gossip) in other towns."

300g/10½ oz plain flour
75g/3oz potato starch or corn flour
75g/3oz icing sugar
1 pinch of salt
2 tablespoons of rum
The seeds of 1 vanilla pod or 1 teaspoon of vanilla
    extract
50g/2oz butter
2 eggs
½ teaspoon yeast
Cooking oil for frying
50g/2oz icing sugar

Put the flour and potato starch on a work surface, make a hole in the centre and add the sugar (using a sieve), salt, vanilla seeds, eggs and rum. Start to bring the flour into the centre, kneading the mixture to create a dough. Add the butter in small pieces (it needs to be cold) and the yeast and mix again until you have a smooth dough.

Sprinkle the work surface and a rolling pin with flour and take a part of the dough (about two fists full) and roll it out as thinly as possible. Continue until all of the dough has been rolled out. Cut into rectangular shapes and make a small slit in the centre of each one.

Fill a frying pan to three-quarters full with cooking oil and heat. Put the galani in the hot oil for a few seconds and remove them with a fork (I take them out two or three at a time), holding them over the pan for a few seconds to allow any excess oil to drain off.

Place the galani on a few sheets of kitchen paper and leave to cool. Once cooled, place the galani in bowls or on a plate and sprinkle with icing sugar.

Treacle Oaties

Dorothy Matthews, Independent Age beneficiary, County Durh[am]

"This recipe is taken from the 13th Whitley Bay Scouts 1936 cookery book, price 1 shilling, passed down to me by my mother. It is still one of my favourite recipes when asked to bake something for the children's club at church."

1 cup flour
1 cup porridge oats
1 tablespoon treacle (or syrup)
170g/6ozs butter (or margarine)
1 cup coconut
1 pinch salt
1 cup sugar
1 tablespoon water
1 teaspoon bicarbonate of soda

Melt the butter and treacle (or syrup). Add the water then the dry ingredients together. Grease a long tin and press the mixture out over the base. Bake at 150°C/gas mark 2 for about 40 minutes. Leave to cool before cutting into fingers.

Dorothy aged three

Damp gingerbread

Jacoba Oldham

"This is a delicious soft gingerbread which is revered by those who are lucky enough to have tried it! It comes from my mother, Susan. The deep freeze bit is essential to get the perfect texture!"

340g/12oz golden syrup
125g/4¼oz margarine
115g/4oz brown sugar
115g/4oz plain flour
140g/5oz self-raising flour
A small teaspoon of bicarbonate of soda
½ tsp ground ginger
egg
280ml/9½ fl oz milk
5 pieces of stem ginger – sliced or coarsely chopped

Mix the egg and milk together well. Place the flour, bicarbonate of soda and ground ginger in a bowl. Melt the golden syrup, sugar and margarine together and allow to cool slightly before pouring onto the dry ingredients in the bowl. Add the egg and milk mixture gradually and pour into a greased and lined loaf tin. Bake in a moderate oven (170°C/gas mark 3) and when the cake mixture is just set, take from the oven and add the stem ginger on to the top. Return loaf to oven. The total baking time for the whole thing should be around 50 minutes. When the gingerbread is cold, place it in the freezer for at least two days.

Lemon drizzle cake

Christine Maa

"I always used to make this cake for volunteer meetings and it flew off the plate. When I stopped, people always missed it, so it has once again worked its way back onto the menu!"

170g/6oz butter or margarine
170g/6oz caster sugar
170g/6oz self-raising flour
2 eggs
Zest of 1 lemon

For the topping:
115g/4oz caster sugar
Juice of 1 lemon

Preheat the oven to 180°C/gas mark 4 and line a loaf tin with greaseproof paper.

Cream the butter and sugar together. Gradually add in the eggs and fold in the flour and lemon zest. Transfer the mixture to the loaf tin and bake for 20-30 mins. Whilst hot, straight from the oven, pour the topping over the top of the cooked cake and leave to cool.

For the topping mix together lemon juice and caster sugar.

Grandma Brown's banana cake

Ros Jenki

"Grandma Brown made banana cake the first time I visited her for tea, in the little cluttered Bath-stone terraced house she'd lived in since she got married. In spite of it being a family favourite, I don't really like bananas. However, Grandma Brown was not the sort of lady who really took no for an answer. Especially about her banana cake."

85g/3oz soft margarine
115g/4oz sugar
1 large egg, beaten
225g/8oz self-raising flour
4 medium bananas, peeled and mashed to a pulp

Plus:
A loaf tin

Preheat the oven to 180°C/gas mark 4. Whisk the sugar, margarine, flour and egg together until they are thoroughly combined. Don't worry if the mixture is dry. Follow with the mashed banana.

Transfer the mixture to a prepared tin and level the top off. Bake in the centre shelf of the oven at a medium heat for 50-55 minutes, until the loaf is golden, well risen and springs back when pressed.

Leave to cool for 10 minutes then loosen around the edges and turn out onto a wire cooling rack to finish cooling.

This cake is nice sliced and spread with butter.

Coconut Cake

Soraya Ebrahimi

I have very fond childhood memories of my grandmother's coconut cake and I never found out how to make it. I developed this coconut cake recipe to recreate those delicious cakes she used to make and they have en going down a storm with my friends and family ever since."

2 cups of good quality, unsweetened desiccated coconut
1 sachet of coconut cream (optional)
1 cup of milk
200g/8oz of margarine
2 cups of caster sugar
2 cups of self-raising flour
½ teaspoon of baking powder
3 eggs
3 drops of vanilla extract

Place the sealed sachet of coconut cream in a cup of hot water to soften the contents to a cream consistency. Place the desiccated coconut, milk and softened coconut cream in a bowl. Mix and leave to stand for at least two hours. Mix occasionally.

In a different bowl cream together the margarine, vanilla extract and sugar. Beat the three eggs in a different bowl and mix into the creamed sugar and margarine, a little at a time. Add the flour and baking powder. Mix together thoroughly. Thoroughly beat in the soaked desiccated coconut mixture.

Transfer the cake mixture into a lined and greased 20cm wide, deep cake tin. Cook in the oven at 160°C/gas mark 3 for 45 minutes and 180°C/gas mark 4 for 20 minutes. If the top starts to brown before the middle is properly cooked, cover the top of the cake with foil and cook on a lower heat in the middle of the oven.

When the top of the cake is brown and your knife is clean when you cut into the centre, remove from the oven and leave to cool.

This recipe can also be made as fairy cakes. These will cook in a 180°C/gas mark 4 oven in approximately 35 minutes.

Chocolate and orange damp cake

Janice Woo

"This is a really decadent cake with a lovely moist texture. I bake it for my family when they come to visit. Try it if you dare!"

150g/5oz good, dark chocolate, melted
350g/12oz dark muscovado sugar
225g/8oz unsalted butter
200g/7oz plain flour
2 eggs, beaten
Grated rind of 1 orange
1 teaspoon bicarbonate of soda
Loaf tin

Preheat the oven to 190°C/gas mark 5. Line the loaf tin with a baking sheet.

Cream the butter and sugar together – with this volume of butter, this is much easier with an electric mixer. Beat in the eggs and orange rind, then, gently fold in the melted chocolate.

Add the bicarbonate of soda to the flour and add this, spoon by spoon to the mixture, alternating each spoon with a spoon of boiling water. Place the mixture, which should be runny, into the loaf tin and bake for 30 minutes followed by a further 15 minutes at 170°C/ gas mark 3.

Leave to cool completely before serving.

Babuffca cake

Agnes Reid, Independent Age beneficiary, Stirli...

"This is a recipe that came from a young student from the Czech Republic. She was studying English and stayed with us for six months. It's best made up in a ring tin, if you have one."

1 mug of sugar
2 mugs of self-raising flour
1 mug of milk
½ mug of cooking oil
1 teaspoon baking powder
1 dessert spoon of drinking chocolate
Plus: large baking tin or ring tin

+2 Eggs !

Mix all of the ingredients together except the drinking chocolate. Put half the mixture into the tin. Gently mix the drinking chocolate into the mixture left in the bowl, then add this to the tin and gently blend to create a marble effect.

Bake in the oven at 180°C/gas mark 4 for 40-45 minutes.

Agnes and her granddaughter

Dolly's fruit cake

Paolo Brand

"One of my favourite memories as a child was eating this cake which dates back to the interwar years. My Nan left us three years ago and this cake is just one of the many memories I have of her."

340g/12oz self-raising flour
170g/6oz granulated sugar
170g/6oz margarine
2 eggs
1 pinch of salt
170g/6oz mixed fruit
A little hot milk mixed with water
1 dessertspoon treacle
½ teaspoon mixed spice

Grease and line an 8-inch deep cake tin.

Put all of the dry ingredients in a bowl and mix together until the margarine is incorporated with the flour. Make a well in the centre of the mix and drop in the eggs, the treacle and a little of the milk and water. Mix until you have a firm texture, adding more milk and water if necessary.

Pour into the prepared cake tin and bake at 160°C/gas mark 3 for 1¾ hours. If the cake is browning too much, then cover loosely with baking paper.

Check after 1½ hours – a skewer should come out clean when inserted into the middle of the cake.

Boiled fruit cake

Pat Hammett, Independent Age beneficiary, Southampt

"You cannot fail with this recipe."

1 cup/mug water
2 cups/mugs of sultanas
1 cup/mug of sugar
115g/4oz margarine
2 teaspoons ginger or mixed spice.
2 eggs
2 cups/mugs of self-raising flour

Put all of the ingredients into a saucepan. Bring to the boil, then lower the heat and simmer for about 10 minutes. Leave to cool for about thirty minutes. Add the eggs and self-raising flour. Mix well and put into a cake tin lined with greaseproof paper.

Cook in the oven at 160°C/gas mark 3 for about 1½ hours. Test the cake with a skewer or knife. If it comes away clean when stuck into the cake, then it's ready.

Granny's specials

Sarah Reed

"This recipe was made up by my mother, Mary Edney, working with what she had in the larder at the time. They immediately became a firm family favourite. They were named 'Granny's specials' by my sister's children after my mother made a batch for them when they came to stay once - and the title stuck.

at them together with a nice cup of tea and a chat."

1 large bar of good quality dark chocolate
1 cup of currants
¾ cup of caster sugar
1 cup desiccated coconut
1 egg
Glacé cherries

Preheat the oven to 190°C/gas mark 5. Cover the bottom of a square metal baking tray with a ¼ inch depth of melted dark cooking chocolate. Cool in the fridge until set.

Mix all the other ingredients apart from the glacé cherries in a bowl. Spread the mixture evenly on top of the cooled chocolate. Dot with glacé cherries to provide one per finished slice.

Bake in the oven until golden on top – about 10-20 minutes, but keep an eye on them.

The Wartime fare that didn't quite make it

" **A**ny book of this nature requires an initial phase of rummaging; of delving through old books, magazines and family scrap books to get a taste of the authentic recipes of the time. There are certain recipes tha instantly spring to mind when one thinks of wartime austerity: Woolton pie, a mixture of whatever vegetables were available with a pastry or potato topping; or perhaps corned beef hash, which assumed the cook could successfully work their way into the tin of the corned beef without the key breaking or cutting their fingers.

But wartime fare went much further than that. And while much of it may seem unglamorous, unappetising even to our modern palate, it is a real testament to the creativity and ingenuity of the cooks and home economists who went to a great deal of trouble to come up with such a varied repertoire on such limited resources.

Many of these authentic recipes have not been included in this book, for no other reason than it is unnecessa to impose the kind of austerity on ourselves now that was simply unavoidable during the time of rationing. The measures imposed on Brits by the British Ministry of Food through the war years were severe but they were a vital part of the war effort. And, as this book aims to show, the main premises were good.

And so, it would be wrong not, at the very least, to give mention to some of the recipes that, although sometimes unappealing, give us a fascinating insight into what our own close relatives; our grandparents and parents would have come to see as the norm. As one child of the war years puts it:

o you mean powdered eggs, bread and dripping? Not everyone suffered. I grew up not knowing any different d had my first banana when I was six. I tried to bite it with its skin still on. Everything was in short supply but made our own fun when and where we could. My mother used to boil up the little bits of soap we now card and cut the result into fresh blocks, darn our socks, mend rips, everything. I cannot recall going hungry food was very basic and even now I have no idea how hard it was for my mother and all the other single ms to put food on the table."

od *Housekeeping* is one of the few publications that continued to be published throughout the War and the od Housekeeping Institute brought out a number of books, helping the British public to create nourishing als in spite of the circumstances.

e *Wartime "Good Housekeeping" cookery book*, compiled by the Good Housekeeping Institute, and published in 42 includes a recipe for wartime pastry, made simply with flour, salt, fat and water – and no eggs. It extols the ues of keeping a stock pot on the go, making use of vegetables and any bones that are leftover, boiling it up a daily basis and emptying only every three to four days.

as a recipe for a meat sauce, using just 4oz of minced meat, which could then be used as the main companiment to flavour rice or noodles or potato pancakes, which were more readily available and filling.

cipes were also available for both eggless batter and one-egg batter, depending on whether or not you were ling flush for eggs that week.

h, *Meat, Egg and Cheese Dishes*, again compiled by the Good Housekeeping Institute and published in 1944, ntains a recipe for mock goose made with ½ lb liver, economical mayonnaise made with one dried egg, and tato pastry, again made with no eggs but, amongst other things, 4oz of dry mashed potato and 2oz of oking fat.

e *Olio cookery book* published in 1948 is a treasure trove of inventive recipes including for example raw beef , which requires you to take ½ lb lean neck of beef, cut it into strips, shred it and place it in a jar with salt, non juice and water, before drinking.

sheep's head pie consists predominantly of one sheep's head and a little ham – reminding you post recipe to e the remainder of the stock for sheep's broth. Indeed, from the same book, it is deemed possible to create ur good meals from one sheep's head. Its game pie without game is made up using 1 lb calf's liver and 1 lb fat con - and a plethora of different herbs for flavouring. And finally, Olio's brain cakes, whose recipe starts quite ply: "remove sheep's brains from sheep's head [and] wash in cold vinegar and water…"

, whether you are making the most of your vegetable patch or taking advantage of the cheaper cuts of meat, hope this cookbook brings a little of the thrift, imagination and fun of the challenge of wartime cooking into e 21st century. Which, perhaps fortuitously, does not include sheep's brain.

Index